WAYS OF TEACHING

WAYS OF TEACHING

JOHN L POWELL

The Scottish Council for Research in Education

SCRE PUBLICATION 89

ISBN 0 947833 06 4

Reprinted in 1992 for the Scottish Council for Research in Education, 15 St John Street, Edinburgh EH8 8JR, by Russell Print, 14 Forrest Street, Blantyre, Glasgow G72 0JP.

CONTENTS

ACKNOWLEDGEMENTS

Although the author accepts full responsibility for the views expressed in this booklet, the views themselves arise from a research programme in which he enjoyed the support of a dedicated research team whose joint discussion of problems produced the insights that it is the function of this booklet to present.

The greatest single debt is owed to Mabel Scrimgeour, who shared with the author the initial conceptualisation of the research. The development of the research methods also owed much to Christine Darroch and James Calderhead. The fieldwork that constituted the final stage of the research was undertaken by Anne Proctor, Finlay Coupar, and Graham McAvoy. The perceptiveness of their observations was of key importance in the interpretation of the data collected. To all the author is deeply grateful.

A further debt is, of course, owed to the teachers who were the subject of the research and who permitted the researchers to observe them in the course of their daily work. They and their schools do, unfortunately, have to remain unnamed in order to preserve their anonymity. (The 'names' of teachers to be found in the text are all fictitious.)

The support of Tayside Region in seconding Mabel Scrimgeour to the research team for the first three years of the project is gratefully acknowledged.

INTRODUCTION

This booklet arises from a SCRE research project, Teaching Strategies in the Primary School. It is not, however, a report on that research: that has already been provided in *The Teacher's Craft* (Powell, J L 1985). Instead it is an attempt on the part of the author to share with teachers some of the understanding that he believes he has derived from being involved in that research. Of course, what is said does not derive solely from that research: his own experience as a teacher has inevitably provided an interpretative background, and what is said and argued is inevitably to some degree personal and subjective. However, the aim of this booklet is not to be didactic—not even when the text contains what amounts to support for particular approaches to teaching; instead it is to encourage teachers to question their own objectives and practices and to aid them in finding for themselves means of improving their teaching in ways that best meet the needs of the pupils they teach.

This is not to say that this booklet, which aims at brevity and simplicity, is a substitute for *The Teacher's Craft*, for the latter not only provides an analytic picture of the teaching undertaken in Scottish primary schools, but provides the reader with an opportunity to explore the evidence and make his own assessment of what support it provides for what is argued both there and in this booklet.

It is not, however, the case that those teachers who read only this booklet need accept its assertions uncritically, for these are open to an important test, that of whether they 'ring true' to their experience as teachers, for although many of the statements may run contrary to some cherished beliefs, they should, if they merit credence, be congruent with the experience of most teachers.

The Research

For the benefit of those who wish to have a brief overview of the research undertaken, a brief outline will be found in the Appendix (p 37). For others, it may suffice to know that the study involved substantial periods of observation of 128 teachers in primary schools distributed over a wide area of Scotland. On the basis of

1

the information obtained in the course of these observations, the teachers were classified in groups such as to bring together for consideration those whose styles of teaching were most similar. References to these groups will be found in the text that follows.

A Note on Gender

The reader will have already noted the use of the masculine pronouns 'he' and 'him' to refer to 'the teacher', even though the reference is meant to teachers of either sex without discrimination. The purpose of so doing is to avoid the repetitive use of 'he/she' and 'him/her'. Only where specific teachers in the project are referred to (anonymously) do the pronouns used reflect whether the teacher in question was male or female.

WAYS OF TEACHING

As has already been explained, the purpose of this booklet is to help teachers in the task of teaching, but it is not a series of prescriptions. Rather it is a basis for thinking afresh about many of the practices commonly adopted by teachers. It thus provides a basis for teachers to look again at their objectives and the ways by which they seek to achieve them.

A broad issue that underlies many narrower ones is the relationship of teaching to learning. Two opposite dangers exist. On the one hand is the danger of the teacher's being so preoccupied with his own activity, teaching, as to give pupils little opportunity to learn: being taught does not necessarily mean that learning occurs. On the other hand is the danger of assuming, because children need to learn, that they are best left to get on on their own, a view that ignores both the need to maintain motivation and to transmit at least some knowledge and concepts. (Children do not have time to rediscover the wheel nor can the transmittible experience of mankind be acquired by a child entirely through his own experience.) This is not to say, however, that the knowledge and concepts can be acquired without some direct personal experience to make them meaningful; nor is it to say that knowledge and understanding are acquired in any real sense unless one has made them 'one's own' by fitting them into, or reconciling them with, the conceptual structures one has already adopted in order to make sense of sensory experience and verbal communication. The process of education is one of continual extension and adaptation of the beliefs and concepts that make up one's view of the world and one's own relationship to it. Although children as well as adults have to make these extensions and adaptations for themselves, they can be helped to do it. It is therefore necessary for every teacher to find ways in which each child can learn in a *variety* of ways. Teaching is, or should be, helping others to learn and to understand.

General principles such as those set out in the immediately preceding paragraphs are of fundamental importance in informing action, but they do not in themselves show what that action should be. The classroom teacher has a practical task involving solving

many problems and reconciling a variety of objectives that may
⌐ ern less than fully compatible with one another.

There is much evidence that different individuals have different
learning styles, or at least different preferred ways of learning.
Nevertheless it is probable that almost everyone learns principally
in four distinct sets of circumstances and benefits from each in
different ways:

1) by receiving information and explanations from others
   seeking to transmit information and/or concepts
2) by interacting with others, arguing out some issue
3) by thinking a problem out for oneself or by seeking to
   apprehend some concept
4) through having direct experience, thus ensuring that
   knowledge and concepts acquired are related to both one's
   sensory experience and to the way one operates in the world.

It is clear that teachers differ considerably in the importance they
attach to these four modes of learning and in the opportunities they
give for them to occur. Moreover, these opportunities differ not
only quantitatively but qualitatively.

Virtually all the teachers observed indicated by their practice that
they considered the first of these modes important, though there
was considerable variation in the extent to which the second was
adopted, for some treated pupil learning as if it were a passive
activity—something like blotting paper (the mind) absorbing ink
(the transmitted knowledge). Others clearly recognised that
anything other than very simple rote learning requires the fitting
together of new and old knowledge, new and old concepts, and that
the old may need to be modified by the new. There was, however,
much variation in the extent to which, if at all, they assisted pupils
to employ one or more of the other three modes of learning that
have been named above. Let us now consider an example.

One of the groups of teachers* consisted of teachers who might
be characterised as being academically able, self-confident, and
individualistic. They 'knew' what their pupils should know and
think, and they set about ensuring that they did know these things
and think these thoughts, *with understanding*. They did not wish
their pupils simply to memorise. To this end, they provided well
reasoned and well ordered exposition of what they wished to teach
and posed questions to their pupils in ways that required them to

* Cluster I in *The Teacher's Craft*.

4

think. (This meant that the pupils had to make call on relevant parts of their existing knowledge and concepts.) They did so in the context of whole-class or large group instruction, for they did not see it as necessary for the learning experience of one pupil to differ from that of another. (This did not, however, preclude their giving additional attention to pupils experiencing difficulty or even providing special attention to those requiring remedial treatment. Nor did it necessarily limit their giving related work of differing difficulty levels or even, in one case, putting up on the blackboard several days' written work to be undertaken by the pupils at their own pace.) They thus gave pupils the opportunity to work in the first two modes listed above but little, if any, of the other two. (The diversity that underlay the characteristics these teachers shared is illustrated in Figure 1.)

What are the implications of their approach, for the work undertaken appeared to 'go well'? They were challenging and treated all that they taught as important and as interesting in its own right, and the pupils appeared to accept their values and to be well motivated. Their pupils typically had training in respect of 'study-skills': study of texts and the use of books of reference readily fitted into the pattern of teaching to which they were exposed. They may even have had a very limited exposure to the third mode of learning in that they may have found it necessary to think out for themselves any point that they had not fully grasped at the time of its exposition, and the fourth, in that they may, occasionally have been asked to recall some specific personal experience. What they certainly did tend to lack was experience of following an argument wherever it might lead: their learning was essentially convergent. To help us see the point of this limitation to what, in other respects seemed outstandingly skilful teaching, let us look at another example, that of a single teacher from another group. Like the teachers that we have just been considering, Mrs Arthur* taught her class either as a whole or in large groups. (Her class was in fact a 'composite' one—a P6/7.) As theirs, her exposition was excellent and her questioning probing and stimulating. Where she differed was in that she was prepared both to exploit any opportunity that arose and to encourage pupils to reach their own conclusions whatever they might be. What was so striking about her pupils was that they were manifestly thinking as they framed their answers. They were encouraged so to do by her

* Teacher 122, Cluster C, in *The Teacher's Craft*. All the names used in this booklet are fictitious and designed to hide the identity of the teachers concerned.

5

Figure 1

Cameos of Three Teachers from the Group described on p 5

*Mr Marshal.** The work of this teacher's class was characterised by the sheer precision with which everything took place. Mr Marshall had a very high level of expectations, and the class responded to them. They were expected to be 'adult' and they were so. He provided a very careful and well thought out introduction to all new work and supplemented the basic instruction given to the class with a good deal of individual instruction. The frequent oral work was stimulating.

There were plenty of reference books available and pupils were encouraged to bring additional materials. Pupils' work-related comments were treated seriously. If a bell for an interval sounded, the class showed no response. Once the teacher was finished, dismissal was orderly and speedy, though without rigid procedures.

Mr McLean. This teacher kept an outstandingly well organised system of individual records of pupils' work, a card being kept for each pupil. The very close check kept on individual progress made it possible for pupils to follow their own programmes. They appeared to be given real responsibility for doing things—such as adjusting the distance of a microphone or in checking the work of other pupils (using, for example, a protractor to check the accuracy of angles).

Miss Broom. This teacher was very well organised and systematic in her teaching. She created a challenging atmosphere but one in which it was possible for lower attaining children to participate. She moreover made substantial demands on the competence and common sense of *all* children. Her system of feedback served the needs of *all*. Although she required some rote learning, she lay equal emphasis on understanding what was learned.

---

* Mr Marshall and the other two teachers described here are Teachers 12, 24 and 89 (cluster 1) in *The Teacher's Craft*. The names used are, of course, fictitious.

refraining from saying that an answer was wrong: instead, if she thought it was not altogether right, she would respond non-committally in a tone that suggested to the pupil that he should go on thinking about what he had just said. In this way pupils were led to find faults in their own responses and amend them. Thus, for children in her class, knowledge and ideas were open-ended, originality was something to be valued, and their own views and interests counted.

It is important to appreciate that learning experience provided by this teacher was substantially different from that provided by the group of teachers we have hitheto been surveying and that the difference had its origin in two different views of the type of learning that should take place. She made full use of all four of our learning modes and, in the process, widened the nature of the learning that occurred.

Both the examples we have considered so far have involved teachers who gave their instruction either to a complete class or to large groups. Some of the others, it is not surprising, taught small groups and indeed organised the work of their classes on the basis of such groups. Does this difference also represent a major difference in approach to teaching? The answer is that *in some cases* it did, but that the ways in which group teaching was employed were too diverse for many unqualified generalisations to be made.

Grouping

50% of the teachers observed normally taught arithmetic to the class as a single unit. A further 20% normally taught two groups separately. The remaining 30% normally taught their classes in three or more groups, though less than half of these had groups of an average size of 7 or less. (The corresponding percentages for English were 61, 21 and 18 respectively). 48% had three or more levels of difficulty for work undertaken in arithmetic (30% in English). Thus the number of difficulty levels did not fully reflect the number of instructional groups: it frequently exceeded it. The level of group activity—as distinct from instruction—is probably best represented by the number of simultaneous activities regularly going on. Approximately one third had two or more for most of the time, but less than 3% had 3-6.

Those who have advocated the use of small groups as the basis for classroom observation and instruction have typically argued that it permits differentiated treatment for pupils and thus the matching of educational provision to individual needs. The evidence of the research was, however, that many of those who employed group methods showed in the way they organised and taught their groups little or no awareness of this objective. Most of the teachers had their classes seated in groups, but the observers very quickly learned that seating arrangements are a very poor guide to whether group methods are indeed being employed at all. Seating arrangements were clearly more sensitive than was teaching practice to teachers' perceptions of orthodoxy—presumably because the former is the more visible.

Instances were not uncommon of pupils seated in circular groups being habitually taught from the blackboard as a single group and of their undertaking written work in ways that would have been no less practicable in the context of traditional rows. Indeed Mrs Arthur (see p 5), who did have her pupils seated in rows, achieved a far greater degree of individualisation of instruction than did many who were employing some form of group teaching. (When one observes classrooms, it is essential to distinguish between what is nominally happening and what is in fact occurring.)

In this context, it is instructive to consider what the difference would have been if, for instance, this same teacher had adopted group methods. What would have been the gains and what the losses? A possible loss would have been of the sustained high level of stimulation that she maintained. Had she worked with groups, as did the other teachers who most resembled her in teaching style, she was unlikely to have been any less stimulating to whichever group she worked with, but she would on average have stimulated any one group for a much shorter time. On the other hand, it would have been easier for her to ensure that *every* pupil was engaged interactively for at least part of the time, and more pupils would have had the opportunity to acquire understanding through personal struggle. All approaches to teaching have to sacrifice some ends in the interest of securing others. Priorities have to be established relative to the children taught — and weaknesses in each approach compensated for as far as possible.

It is unfortunately the case, however, that the adoption of whole-class (or large-group) teaching does not guarantee stimulation and that small group methods do not guarantee either differentiation of work to meet individual needs or the opportunity for pupils to be actively involved in making ideas and facts 'their own'. The potential benefits of either approach are achieved by the skills brought to bear by teachers—but unfortunately not by all teachers.

Where failure to achieve the characteristic virtues of group teaching—notably differentiation of activity to match individual needs and the opportunity for *all* pupils to learn actively and co-operatively—occurs, it is, the experience of the research suggests, largely due to one or both of two factors:

i) that the teacher employs group methods because it is the conventional wisdom that they should be used and not because of being committed to, or even understanding, their purposes, and

ii) that they lack the necessary organisational skill, and perhaps also prepare inadequately.

It was clear from the research that the number of teachers was small who used group methods in ways that secured from those methods advantages that it is difficult or impossible to obtain otherwise. Mr McDonald* is, perhaps, the best example that can be cited from this research of a teacher who had not only found a solution to the central problem of how to distribute his own time when having a class working in groups but had established groups that worked as cooperative units: he worked with individual groups in a stimulating way, he ensured that all groups could organise activities for themselves and be self-supporting, he ensured that they had interesting tasks to undertake, and he did not require them to work alone for periods longer than they could sustain. (He in fact had some activities conducted on a whole-class basis and thus eased his task of maintaining interest and motivation.)†

In contrast, classes in which group methods were employed unprofitably were characterised by

a) over-involvement of the teacher in a limited range of tasks, such as correction, and/or

b) pupils' being left for long periods either doing repetitive work, or 'stuck' with a problem, or simply unmotivated, and/or

c) failure to provide a range of interesting tasks and/or material to carry them out, and/or

d) lack of training of pupils in organising their own time and in undertaking for themselves responsibilities that otherwise fall on an over-burdened teacher.

It is not being argued here that the solution adopted by Mr McDonald is the only one available; nor is it necessarily an ideal. Many other practices may contribute to solving the organisational problems of group teaching. Thus, for example, a teacher may 'stagger' new work, so that only one or two groups are at any one time at a stage where the personal involvement of the teacher may

* Teacher 106 (cluster A), in *The Teacher's Craft*.

† A fuller description of this teacher is contained in Figure 2.

9

Figure 2

Cameo of Mr McDonald*

Mr McDonald taught his class principally in groups, but for parts of the day they were brought together to operate as a single unit.

He made it a primary objective that the groups should learn to work self-reliantly on their own when he was busy working with one particular group. To assist them to do so, he ensured that all materials and resources they would need were readily available for them to take and that each was clearly labelled. (By prior preparation, he had, in this respect, made up for his non-availability at the time.)

It was particularly notable how his pupils worked together in their groups. If, for example, when he had been discussing a passage of text with a group, he asked the group 'to ask each other questions', they did so enthusiastically. Moreover, individual pupils were observed to take over spontaneously the teaching/management of their groups: the others put up their hands when they had something to contribute, thus trusting this pupil as the teacher.

Because he devoted himself fully to whichever group he was working with, he was not available to others at times of their choosing. That he did in fact ensure in advance that they had a clear programme to follow was clearly a matter of basic importance. Probably no less important was the fact that he did not leave them to themselves for longer than they could manage: bringing the class together as a single group provided fresh stimulation to all.

If any inappropriate behaviour did occur, his response was likely to be blunt:

> 'Frank, that's a disgrace: everybody else keeps their books in order, so why can't you?'

However, the underlying positive relationship between him and the class meant that he could be blunt without souring relationships. Indeed, he seemed to be building up the social and academic confidence of a class whose social background was far from privileged.

Although Mr McDonald had clearly found viable solutions to many of the problems experienced by teachers instructing their classes on a small group basis, he showed no complacency and certainly did not see himself as notably successful. He saw the teaching situation as one constantly presenting new or old problems, and their solution as equally constantly commanding his thinking.

His willingness to see teaching as a problem-solving activity, one where problems have to be analysed, was probably one of his most valuable characteristics.

---

* Teacher 106 (cluster A) in *The Teacher's Craft*.

be required for substantial periods; activities for different groups can be scheduled such that ones requiring much teacher involvement and ones requiring virtually none coincide; combining self-correcting facilities with good record keeping can both reduce the time the teacher has to devote to marking and, at the same time, permit monitoring of individual progress; and a breakdown service can be organised to provide aid to pupils who have failed to overcome their own problems. Moreover, a class may have a more 'fluid' way of working than Mr McDonald's, with the result that there is greater emphasis on individual pupils' doing what is necessary for themselves—perhaps by moving to wherever a particular task can best be undertaken, something that in practice may involve the spontaneous formation of temporary groups.

It is important to take note of the fact that but few of the teachers observed who were employing group methods were, even if their organisation of their own time was satisfactory, doing so in ways that afforded advantages unobtainable through whole-class (or large-group) instruction, and that the more skilled of the teachers employing whole-class (or large-group) instruction secured *by different means* at least some of the advantages—eg, in respect of individualisation—normally associated with group methods. Indeed, it might be argued that those who failed to overcome the problems specific to small-group methods would have lost little, if anything, had they abandoned them in favour of a less demanding approach. (For an example of group methods failing to achieve their purposes, see Figure 3.)

Unfortunately, the evidence of the research also shows quite clearly that the successes of the most able 'whole-class' teachers were not shared by all those who instructed their classes on the whole-class basis. Weakness in teaching skills, poor feedback, dullness, excessive allocation of time to work so repetitive as to serve little function other than that of keeping pupils occupied, and failure to identify and respond to individual differences—all matters to which we shall return—were found both where group methods were employed and where they were not. Queues of pupils waiting for correction of their work, time-wasting transitions from one task to another, and lack of pupil-training to permit them to operate efficiently without constant direction are, alas, found in both situations.

Simon and Galton* have argued on the basis of the ORACLE

* Galton M and Simon B (ed), *Progress and Performance in the Primary Classroom*, Routledge and Kegan Paul, London, 1980.

11

Figure 3

A Cameo of Mrs Underwood*

Mrs Underwood was notable for the very large number of separate activities occurring simultaneously in her class, for her responsiveness to pupils' interests, for her efforts to allow each child to work at his own level, for her working with individuals for substantial periods of time, for her encouragement of co-operation at least at times, for her skilled matching of responsibilities to pupil needs, and for the very marked informality of her relationships with her pupils. However, the efficiency of her management was below that of other teachers in her group and, despite her informality, she was somewhat coercive. In attempting to achieve her ends, she tried to be everywhere at once. The result was considerable under-employment of pupils and a lack of application on the part of some of them. In view of the unrealistic demands that she placed on herself, it is not surprising that the observer noted that she was 'sometimes irritated' by the demands the class made on her.

_____

* Teacher 5 (cluster N) in *The Teacher's Craft.*

study—*which involved studies of teaching employing observations instruments that differed from SCOTS† in concentrating attention on narrower aspects of the teaching process—that there is a need to maximise inter-action between teachers and pupils, that this can best be done by employing whole-class teaching, and that group methods can profitably be used in conjunction with such whole-class teaching. (Wholly individualised instruction they rejected on the grounds that, unless classes are extremely small, adequate teacher-pupil interaction can in no way be achieved.) The findings of the research described in this book lend general support to this view, but it is important to remember that many of the problems that teachers have to solve exist wholly independently of whether whole-class, group, or individualised approaches are employed. It is, therefore, to issues that inform and underlie these problems that we must now devote attention.*

Operation of Systems

No teacher can operate a class as an efficient organisation

† The observation schedule (System for the Classroom Observation of Teaching Strategies) used in the research described in this booklet.

without the active and informed participation of the pupils in operating whatever system the teacher decides to adopt. It was manifest to the observers that in well-run classes the pupils knew what was expected of them, knew how to proceed in various circumstances, could operate effectively for periods of time even in the absence of the teacher, and, because they did not have to make many enquiries of the teacher about how to proceed or about how to overcome routine problems, left the teacher free to teach or interact with individuals or groups as proved necessary. This knowledge of procedures did not come by chance: the classes concerned had been informed of these procedures and trained in operating them at the very beginning of their time with their current teacher. It is of fundamental importance therefore that teachers should have well thought-out operational procedures. There is no purpose served in a teacher's giving the same instructions or making unvarying decisions day in, day out. Instead he should ensure early in the school year that pupils are familiar with procedures and know how to operate them. Only in this way can a teacher optimise the use of his own time and avoid constant involvement in trivia. Indeed it was noticeable that, in classes where pupils had not been trained to manage for themselves even minor problems, the teachers were overwhelmed with trivial enquiries and pupils wasted much time while awaiting attention.

Direct and Indirect Control

What is indirect control, and how does it operate? Getting pupils to learn and operate procedures—as advocated in the preceding section—is, once established, of course, a form of indirect control. Providing activities and materials that are at the pupils' disposal is another, for, although the pupils may be able to choose amongst these, the menu offered is, in fact, in the control of the teacher.

It is of course a fallacy to suppose that teachers have an option of renouncing all control in order to allow pupils to follow their own bent. (For a teacher to abrogate control is to renounce all responsibility for the education of the pupils entrusted to him.) The real options lie in how control is exercised and particularly in whether it is effected directly or indirectly. In the short term at least, direct control is the easier to implement, for there is an exact and obvious relationship between the instruction given and the desired effects. On the other hand, direct instruction has some inherent disadvantages:

13

a) it involves action by the teacher at every step or transition and this makes more frequent demands on the teacher's time than may be necessary

b) both ends and means are *overtly* dictated to pupils

c) pupils are, therefore, the less likely to adopt the teacher's ends as their own.

It would be unwise to over-stress the last of these points since this research affords numerous instances of classes apparently accepting wholly imposed means and ends. On the other hand, there were many instances of pupils working without enthusiasm, and a few of classes where a substantial proportion of the pupils were either apathetic or even hostile to the teacher's objectives. It is clearly essential that, by one means or another, every class broadly share the teacher's objectives.

Some would argue that this can best be achieved by giving pupils real choice in what they do. However, there are obvious dangers that pupils' choices will be based on criteria that ignore their long-term interests, if only because they lack any basis for knowing what their long-term interests are, and teachers are, in any case, rarely willing to forego control. What is commonly forgotten, however, is that the giving of pupil choice does not necessarily imply the renouncement of teacher control. For this there are two principal reasons. The first is that by skilfully structuring the context in which pupil choice is exercised, teachers can influence very heavily indeed the choices made. The second is that the options offered to pupils can all be compatible with the fulfilment of the teacher's objectives. In short, pupils may choose freely, or at least have the impression of choosing freely, while remaining effectively under teacher control. For them to have that impression may be important, for a sense of involvement in where they are going may very well be a major factor in avoiding the development of pupil disaffection, especially in the longer term. However, it has to be noted that there were many instances of pupils' displaying obvious involvement despite the lack of exercise of choice. (Only about 16% of teachers encouraged pupils to choose, but only about half of these enthusiastically. 33% of the teachers determined the work undertaken without a semblance of pupil participation.)

It is particularly important to realise that pupil choice does not need to be individual: a discussion leading to consensus concerning, say, a topic for discussion can give the pupils a feeling that what they are doing is what they have jointly chosen to do. On the other hand, it is equally important to realise that nominal choices where all the options pre-determined by the teacher seem equally unattractive (as can, for example, be the case where a choice of essentially similar work-cards is offered) do not confer the advantages usually associated with the exercise of choice.

A specific instance of a practice where many of these issues arise is that of the so-called 'integrated day/week', where work to be undertaken by pupils during a pre-determined period—eg, a day or week—is set down, usually on a blackboard. (Approximately 8% of the classes operated in this way.) A common supposition is that this not only permits pupils to work at their own pace and motivates them to work hard so that they may move on to optional activities of their own choice, but allows them to exercise effective choice. While this supposition is well-founded in certain instances, it is frequently not so, for often the teacher requires the work to be undertaken in a pre-determined order and the only variation amongst pupils is in pace of working. Often it is manifest that the integrated day/week is used simply as a means of exerting pressure on pupils to complete a set amount of work in a given time, the penalty for non-completion being deprivation from participation in some generally preferred activities and/or a requirement to do unfinished work at home. Thus here too appearances may be deceptive.

In the extreme case where control is not only direct but total, it has to be recognised that the issues are no longer just those of interest and motivation, but of initiative. If a pupil has no opportunity to initiate or redirect work or discussion, his role is necessarily a purely responsive one. Thinking and learning cease to be processes in which he is actively involved: he is but echoing a thinking process that is active only in the teacher's mind.

Motivation

Choice, even if apparent rather than real—and indeed anything that leads to a sharing of objectives by teacher and class—is clearly an important means of securing pupils' motivation. However, the research drew attention to other means by which motivation can be established and maintained.

One such way that has already been mentioned is to exploit opportunities—eg, a chance event or some matter happening to arise in the course of class work—by abandoning planned work for the meantime and pursuing the matter of interest while interest is still aroused. Such exploitation of opportunities, however, pre-supposes an appropriate attitude of mind in the class teacher and the possession of a wide range of knowledge that can be called on on the spur of the moment. But rewards can be considerable: the shared enthusiasms that are generated by exploiting interests help to produce in classes a sense of one-ness that encompasses the teacher as well as the pupils. (For a further example of exploiting opportunities, see Figure 4.)

Figure 4

Cameo of Miss Finlay*

Miss Finlay taught in a school whose pupils were drawn from a notably under-privileged background. Her P5 class had during the previous year—when it had another teacher—been seriously out of control. Miss Finlay had, therefore, to secure, and ensure the continuance of, her own control, as well as teach her pupils fundamental work skills—they worked in groups—and to develop better attitudes to school and learning. Their interest span nonetheless remained short and she was particularly adept at regaining their interest by introducing abrupt changes in work when she sensed it was necessary. This sometimes involved pursuing some topic that had arisen largely by chance but which was clearly interesting her pupils. This is not to say that the work pursued was random. She was skilled at turning such occasions to her own purposes.

* Teacher 38 (cluster C) in *The Teacher's Craft*.

Another important means of maintaining motivation is reinforcement of desired conduct by ensuring that it is regularly praised. However, the observations made it clear that while the opposite—habitual criticism—was in some cases either a demotivating or alienating factor, even sharp criticism of pupil work did not necessarily demotivate. Much seemed to depend on the basic relationship between teacher and class: a teacher who was liked by the class or perceived of as generally well-disposed to the class could criticise bluntly either work or conduct without causing offence and consequent demotivation. Indeed, self-confident and able pupils were noted to be stirred to fresh effort by sharp criticism. It appeared to be in recognition of this fact that some teachers differentiated their comments such that the able incurred criticism and the less able, encouragement. (To the whole issue of the use of praise, we shall return later.)

16

It is important to recognise the existence of two sorts of motivation, *extrinsic* and *intrinsic*. The former—rewards of one sort or another, including marks, points, stars, etc.—involves: 1) the establishment of a system which arouses in the pupils the desire to have the rewards on offer and, 2) subsequently, some decisions as to when to bestow the rewards—something that gives rise to issues similar to those we shall later discuss when we come to consider the role of praise. Intrinsic motivation, on the other hand, lies in the satisfaction that may be obtained from undertaking the work. Not least important here is the teacher's own attitude to the work. Work or learning that appears to bore the teacher is unlikely to arouse pupil interest. (4% of the teachers observed were thought to be listless and unenthusiastic about their teaching). A lively personality is an obvious asset for a teacher in respect of arousing and maintaining interest, but some teachers who must have appeared to their pupils as very "serious" individuals were able to evoke interest be means of clear presentation of ideas and arguments. Some did, of course, try to relate work to topics or events of known interest to pupils, but there was abundant evidence that this was by no means a pre-requisite. (About 21% of the classes observed appeared to derive motivation from the work undertaken rather than from "rewards"; about 23% depended largely on extrinsic rewards. Save for 5% of classes that appeared largely unmotivated, the remainder represented a mixture of intrinsic and extrinsic motivation.)

Competition

Competition amongst pupils is usually used by teachers as a means of motivating pupils to greater effort, though some teachers avoid it out of fear that the less able will be discouraged and demotivated through constant failure. Many pupils do clearly enjoy competing with each other. The researchers indeed had their attempt to develop a test (one of application to a repetitive task) proved invalid when a class on which the materials were being piloted spontaneously turned the various stages of the test, designed to measure differential fall in work-rates, into a race! (See *The Teacher's Craft*, p.132)

What the researchers found particularly interesting was the different ways in which competition was employed by different teachers. Where competition was used in a light-hearted way, most pupils appeared to enjoy it and it is open to much doubt whether the less successful were in any way damaged by it. Where the

17

competition was conducted in a more serious, more 'cut-throat' way, that some might be damaged by the experience seemed an altogether more plausible possibility. Instances of intense 'cut-throat' competition were, however, extremely rare (less than 3%).

There was, however, another quite different sort of competition to be found in some other classes; in this the pupils competed only with themselves, seeking to do better, not than others, but than they themselves had previously done. (This was characteristic of 37% of the classes observed. In 60% of the classes no competitive element was detected other than in games.)

Pressure to Secure Work

Instead of, or as well as, motivating their pupils to work, many teachers exert some degree of pressure on them. The extent of this pressure was, indeed, something that the researchers endeavoured to observe and record. In the event, they found that when the pressure was overt—ie, through punishment or the threat of it, rebuke, the meaningful look etc.—it was relatively easy to record. However, they realised that psychological pressure, though detectable or at least inferrable, could not reliably be assessed. The very presence of some teachers clearly exerted great pressure on pupils to work. How their dominance had been achieved it was impossible to tell: what was obvious was that it was established and unquestioned.

Another form of pressure that was less than fully overt was exercised by some teachers by requiring all work to be completed, if necessary at home or at times when other pupils were being allowed to pursue activities that they enjoyed and/or had chosen.

Some might fear that pressure is psychologically damaging to pupils. Although the research did not attempt to measure psychological effects, it did appear very unlikely that all the pressure observed was harmful. Where consistent and effective pressure was exerted and resulted in unquestioning compliance, the pupils' lives seemed at least to be free of conflict. Where there was conflict and/or where pupils felt unjustly treated, the possibility of psychological damage appeared a more open question.

About 16% of classes were thought to be under strong or fairly strong 'overt' pressure.

The Role of Praise

Some reference has already been made (see p 16) to the use of praise to increase motivation. To the observers there seemed to be

18

little doubt that a warm, supportive atmosphere did incline pupils to be co-operative. But the warmth did have to be *genuine*. Pupils are highly perceptive, and mechanical praise does not create a warm atmosphere. What appeared to count was the basic attitude of the teacher to the class: if this was deemed by the class to be benign, much else would be tolerated or, if necessary, forgiven. The teacher who was liked and could be seen to be well disposed could indeed criticise bluntly and have the criticism accepted. On the other hand, criticism that was seen as unfair, and particularly criticism habitually focussed on particular pupils whom the teacher could be inferred to dislike, seemed commonly to alienate not only those criticised but the class as a whole.

Being aware of factors such as these may assist teachers to avoid blunders, but the fundamental lesson would seem to be that the teacher who is to be seen as well disposed must *be* well-disposed. Praise, in these circumstances, will arise naturally from the attitude and not be a matter of mere technique or of conscious manipulation.

There is, however, another possible function of praise to be considered, its use as a 'reward' designed to reinforce desired behaviour. The idea is a simple one: if satisfactory work is done or satisfactory conduct occurs, and if it is rewarded—with praise or by some other means—it is more likely to be repeated. (Whether undesired behaviour is more likely to be 'extinguished' if it is ignored than if it receives 'negative reinforcement'—viz punishment or deprivation of reward—has, of course, long been a contentious issue.)

The research undertaken did not resolve these issues—nor did it attempt to do so—but it did reveal that the implementation of practices that have their theoretical basis in such theories is less straightforward than may commonly be supposed. Let us ask some questions about possible effects of a teacher's praising a piece of work that has been done by a pupil. Does the pupil conclude—

 a) that the work is poor?
 b) that the teacher likes him?
 c) that the praise means nothing in particular?

The answers to these questions will, in any particular instance, depend on a number of factors such as—

 i) whether the pupil believes that the work deserves the praise,
 ii) whether the teacher normally confers praise on others only

when it seems deserved or whether his praise is routine and undiscriminating?

iii) whether the teacher sounds sincere and/or whether he gives convincing reasons for his praise,

iv) the pupil's general assessment of the teacher's attitude to him.

How criticism will be reacted to is likely to depend on the same or analagous factors.

No doubt, in general, criticism undermines confidence and diminishes motivation, and praise does the reverse. But there is a big difference between a tendency and a universal relationship. The criticism that may damage still further the confidence and motivation of a child who seldom achieves success may spur to fresh effort a normally successful and self-confident one. The praise that one child may enjoy may embarrass another, and run off the back of yet another. Even for the same child, the effect of praise may depend on circumstances: private praise may give pleasure, public praise may embarrass (by damaging standing in the eyes of peers or by reinforcing a reputation for being a teacher's pet). Even two instances of public praise of the same pupil may be different in effect: whereas what is seen (by class and pupil) as biassed praise may be embarrassing to the pupil concerned, unexpected and spontaneous praise by the teacher of a good idea advanced by a pupil may please that pupil and win the admiration of at least most of the class.

Teachers do of course learn from experience about the effects of praise (or blame), at least in some highly specific ways—eg. that praising (or blaming) a particular pupil or group of pupils is counterproductive. Unfortunately such learning is seldom systematic and seldom includes those pupils who do not manifest their reactions strongly or who keep them covert. To be aware of the effects he is having on his pupils is a key responsibility of any teacher. Observation of teachers in their classrooms shows that many teachers take this responsibility very seriously, but it also reveals clearly that many—whether through indifference, insensitivity, or lack of perceptiveness—fail to appreciate adequately the effects they are having on their pupils and thus fail to achieve their objectives.

It is important to distinguish clearly between praise and feedback. Telling a pupil that an answer is correct or that what he has done is satisfactory (or good) is necessary feedback, but it should not be regarded as "praise" for the purposes of the present discussion. Praise is here taken to mean something over and above feedback. (A pupil may, of course, be pleased by favourable feedback and his efforts reinforced by it, but it should be remembered that praise is something that can be bestowed whether it is merited or not.) This distinction between praise and feedback is stressed by Jere Brophy in the course of a very valuable and perceptive summary and discussion of the findings of a large of number of research projects.*

The following points are derived from Brophy's article, but it should be noted that they are fully consistent with the experience and judgement of the researchers involved in the project on which this booklet is based:

(1) Praise does not necessarily act as a reinforcer of learning and/or desirable conduct, and it certainly will not do so if the pupil is unclear about exactly what is being praised and unless he perceives the praise as being genuine.

(2) Some pupils do not like being praised. This is particularly likely to be so when, or if, they think it brings them into disrepute with their peers. In any case, praise is likely to be valued only if it comes from a teacher who is esteemed. "Rather than assume the effectiveness of praise, teachers should monitor students for their apparent reaction to it."

(3) Many pupils who like being praised by their teachers are skilful at eliciting praise from them. Such pupils may bring work to teachers specifically to be praised for it, and many may even overtly seek praise. In particular, they tend to reward teachers for their praise by indicating their pleasure at receiving it (eg. by smiling). Praising such pupils may improve the general atmosphere of the class but its effect on work is likely to be unspecific. Moreover these are the very pupils teachers are least likely to find it necessary to reinforce or motivate. Most—though not all—of these pupils are self-motivated. Those of them who really need help also need good diagnosis/feedback/special teaching.

(4) Those pupils who perform poorly and/or lack self-confidence may be helped by praise, but even for them the praise must be credible. Pupils who see themselves as singled out for praise they know they have not merited may take the praise as confirmation of their own inadequacy. Such pupils are most

* *Review of Educational Research*, 51,1 (AERA, Washington 1981).

likely to be helped if they receive good feedback and praise for *genuine*, if small, improvements.

(5) Most teachers praise (as distinct from giving positive feedback) fairly seldom. This is not necessarily a bad thing. Fair evaluation is likely to be appreciated by most pupils. Those teachers who praise a lot and do so warmly and convincingly probably have their main effect through creating a warm, co-operative atmosphere rather than by providing reinforcement. Those who praise (or blame) a lot, but perfunctorily, are likely to have a negligible effect thereby.

(6) Criticism can be seen as negative praise—though constructive criticism need not be so. Constant purposeful criticism is obviously liable to undermine pupil confidence. Teachers need to judge how much criticism each pupil can take and respond positively to. (Many able/successful pupils may prefer constructive criticism to fulsome praise and many can take even sharp but merited criticism in their stride.)

(7) Praise for conduct is most usually directed to well-behaved pupils who would in any case behave well. No doubt such praise is commonly intended "pour encourager les autres", but there is little evidence of its being effective. (Such pupils are unlikely to be envied or admired by their less law-abiding class-mates!) Using praise to reinforce good conduct in troublesome pupils is likely to have very limited success *in the classroom situation*. (It is Brophy's view that behaviour-modifiers' techniques for extinguishing undesirable behaviours and reinforcing desirable ones are usable only in a one-to-one situation. The closeness of observation and the accuracy of (repeated) response needed by the modifier is too great for a teacher to provide in a normal classroom situation.)

All that has been said here concerning the use of praise points yet again to the obvious truth that good teaching practice requires a good deal of "common sense", a good deal of putting oneself in the position of each type of pupil and trying to look at one's actions and hear one's own words through their eyes and ears. A little well-directed praise is worth more than a lot of thoughtless praise. (All but the youngest pupils are likely to judge words and actions very perceptively.)

Teachers' skilful questioning to elicit good answers from pupils is likely to be more valuable than their praising answers, for good questioning helps pupils to see for themselves when they are answering well. Self-evaluation can produce self-reinforcement. Pupils can be further helped in self-evaluation by being helped to set appropriate goals and to recognise when they have attained them. In short, teacher-praise is no substitute for teacher-skill supported by teacher-warmth.

Relationships between Teacher and Pupils

It has already been demonstrated in an earlier section that teacher-pupil relationships have a bearing on how pupils react in various circumstances. There appear, however, to be two partially related aspects of such relationships. The first aspect relates to the formality/informality of the relationships and the second to the similarity/disparity of social background, interests, etc.

Extreme informality, where pupils treated the teacher as a social equal, was confined to a very small number of teachers (less than 2%). This informality did not appear to result in the teacher's enjoying notable popularity, though it has to be said that this may have been due less to the informality itself than to other characteristics such as irritability when over-extended or an unwillingness to be bothered with the less able. It has also to be noted that many teachers who were obviously very well-liked by their pupils did maintain a well-defined social distance between themselves and their pupils. There is, however, a clear distinction to be drawn between the degree of social distance that may command respect and that which implies indifference or even hostility. The latter (which was confined to about 8% of those observed) typically caused pupils to keep their distance or, where the teacher also tended to be hostile (less than 2%), themselves to display hostility.

Disparity of social background between teacher and class can, of course, make it more difficult for the two to share interests, and, moreover, may possibly make it more difficult for the pupils to see the teacher as having characteristics that it would be good to emulate. Disparity of social background is obviously likely to be most acute in schools where the pupils are drawn from severely socially under-privileged backgrounds. Mr Hughes*, who not only lived in the same underprivileged area as his pupils but spoke with the same accent, used similar speech patterns, and shared with them some non-standard usages (such as 'he done it'.) This teacher certainly had a good relationship with his class, but whether the

* Teacher 39 (cluster B) in *The Teacher's Craft*.

23

fact that his style of speech—and, by inference, his social background—was not notably different from theirs did in any significant way contribute to their good relationship or indeed to their willingness to learn, it was not possible to glean. It is probably futile for a teacher to attempt to imitate the speech, interests, and ways of a cultural background other than his own, but the need to understand differences of outlook stemming from different cultural backgrounds seems obvious.

Developing Pupil Responsibility

Almost all the teachers seemed concerned that their pupils should display a responsible attitude to their school work. Rather fewer appeared to be equally concerned about helping them to become adults with a sense of responsibility.

Some of those who did little to develop pupil responsibility (about 9%) clearly viewed their pupils as being in any case irresponsible and untrustworthy and as unlikely to develop responsibility. That their own manifest distrust might in fact induce irresponsible behaviour in their pupils was something of which they showed no awareness.

Where distrust was at its greatest (less than 3%), fear of disorder appeared to be the major reason for giving pupils virtually no duties to perform. In other less extreme instances, duties might be given but were supervised so closely as to deny any genuine responsibility to the pupils executing them.

Those who did give pupils responsibilities fell into three broad categories. The first encompasses those who trusted pupils to behave responsibly and saw the giving of responsibility as a means of promoting it (approximately 16%). (The trust of such teachers did not appear to be abused even by pupils who were known to have been a source of trouble to a teacher in the preceding year, though this finding could be explained in terms of those whose trust had been abused having ceased to trust.) The second category includes those teachers who gave out responsibilities – usually on a rota basis—but placed clear limits on the extent of their trust (a further 45%). Those in the third category (30%) gave responsibilities only to those seen as both competent and keen: in short they appeared to be interested in exploiting the assistance of those who could be depended upon to act responsibly rather than in developing responsibility in the remainder.

There seemed to be some evidence that teacher training had done more to communicate the techniques by which responsibilities could be widely distributed—eg, duty rosters—than to impart understanding of how responsibility might be developed.

It has already been implied that responsible attitudes are likely to be promoted only by the exercising of real responsibility and that trust is a pre-requisite thereof. Many teachers were obviously much concerned to establish in pupils the standards they expected of them, and, provided only that the relationship between teacher and pupils was such that the pupils wished to gain the teacher's good regard, this appeared to be a generally effective strategy.

The most extreme instance of a real responsibility being given was when a teacher entrusted a pupil with the task of telephoning a local authority adviser to obtain some information useful to the class. However, although opportunities at that level can seldom be procured, duties, such as managing a class library, that depend for their success on conscientious application can be found. Giving pupils freedom to move around the room for acceptable purposes and giving them free access to all, or almost all, materials and equipment obviously provides an opportunity for all regularly to learn to behave with responsibility.

It can, of course, be readily accepted that not all pupils are capable of accepting some higher levels of responsibility and that there is a need to match task to individual. This some teachers did with considerable skill and they were, moreover, prepared to help those who most needed to develop responsible attitudes. Having a changing rota of duties helped to share out responsibilities, but it was much more valuable when thought was given by the teacher to how it should be made up.

Teacher Knowledge and Skills

a) *Knowledge* The background of knowledge that the teachers brought to their tasks varied very greatly. The most knowledgeable were clearly persons of high ability and wide interest and were able to provide informed comment on virtually any topic that arose. At the other extreme were those who were clearly ill-informed and who communicated to their pupils inaccurate information. Some of them were, unfortunately, also inclined to be dogmatic—and to be unwilling to look up what they were unsure about. (See Figure 5.)

It was possible to ascertain that amongst teachers who were themselves most knowledgeable in many spheres were some who showed weaknesses in respect of numeracy. These teachers were typically well aware of their weaknesses, but their reaction was frequently to minimise the time they spent on arithmetic in order to be able to spend more time on activities where they felt more secure.

While it would be foolish to argue that extent of knowledge is the major factor in teacher quality, inadequacy of knowledge is something for which other skills and qualities cannot wholly compensate. It is important that weakness in important areas such as numeracy should be detected and rectified during pre-service training.

Figure 5

When the Teacher Doesn't Know*

Some teachers endeavour to be the sole source of knowledge. This is particularly unfortunate when they are not themselves well-informed. Mrs Young, an observer noted 'would give the wrong answer rather than consult a book'. Of Miss George it was noted: 'Pupils may be wary of how they reply to questions as she is likely to ridicule them—this seems all the more extreme when she has her facts wrong'.

---

* The teachers referred to are Teachers 110 and 71 (cluster M) in *The Teacher's Craft*.

---

b) *Teaching Skill* Since almost universally the first step when a teacher seeks to introduce new work to a class or group is some form of presentation of facts and ideas, skill in exposition is clearly of fundamental importance. (Even when 'discovery methods' are employed, there is, in the presentation of the problem and the materials and in the way the teacher responds to pupils' attempts, some sort of implied exposition.) Exposition does not, of course, necessarily imply the teacher's making statements: the teacher may, for instance, pose questions and the pupils attempt to provide the statements. But, whatever the precise process adopted, unless the teacher is providing some structuring of the knowledge, he is contributing little to the pupils' learning. Obviously, however, if a teacher does not have sufficient understanding of what he is seeking to teach to be able to provide a useful structure, he inevitably fails in this vital step. This then is a point at which the teacher's knowledge and depth of understanding of subject matter is almost certain to be of crucial importance.

However, even a well-structured piece of teaching is unlikely to achieve immediate and sustained learning by every pupil. In any case, new learning has to be related to old, and the old is unlikely to be the same for all pupils either in respect of knowledge or of structuring. The teacher may therefore need to explore the interface between what he is seeking to teach and what the individual pupil already knows. Much may depend on his ability to see the current situation through each pupil's eyes, so that old and new knowledge and structures may interlock, and then perhaps to find an alternative structuring of what has been already taught. It is at this second stage that teachers appear most often to fail: many seem to be able to find one structure—not necessarily an optimal one—but not two. Those teachers who found it difficult to teach a topic in more than one way would be likely to benefit from specific training designed to enhance their skills in the structuring and restructuring of ideas and associated information.

It must be stressed that ability to structure is unlikely to be independent of knowledge and understanding of what has to be structured, but flexibility of approach to a single topic is something that it may be possible to foster.

The same flexibility is likely to be helpful to teachers in enabling them to recognise different learning styles in pupils and either to adapt presentations to those learning styles or to seek to modify the learning styles themselves.

Sometimes the different approach may be found by individual pupils, though this, it must be said, did not appear to be common. Unfortunately, the observers found that only 22% of the teachers observed encouraged pupils in this and that 12½% refused to accept any approach other than their own. The remainder at most tolerated any originality on the part of pupils. The teachers who sought to have pupils adopt their ways were doubtless convinced that their ways were best—and they may well have been so. The point at issue is not what it may be best to learn but what may be the best way of learning. The pupil who has "got the right answer the wrong way" may have more understanding than the one who has meekly followed instructions. If the pupil's own thinking has led him astray, the teacher's task is surely to help him find his way to a better path? Independent thinking by pupils is, surely, something to be encouraged?

Questioning

Questioning can serve a wide variety of purposes. It may, for instance, be designed to do no more than test the recall of something that should have been memorised or even only to secure attention. Our concern here is, however, with questioning directed to more substantial ends.

One of the commonest markers of an inexperienced teacher is answering his own questions. His doing so may betray some degree of insecurity, but more often it indicates that the questions are no more than disguised statements. The teacher, having made up his mind what he wants to say, wants an immediate simple and direct answer that effectively puts into a pupil's mouth exactly what he himself wishes to say. If he does not get the answer quickly, he feels unable to wait, and he betrays that his desire is to tell, rather than to give pupils the opportunity to learn. The questions he asks, when such are his aims, are, of course, likely to amount to requests for simple recall rather than for thinking.

Most teachers learn to be more persistent, but not necessarily to question better. Higher level questioning typically requires the pupil to arrive at a response either through reasoning or through selection of the most relevant of a number of recalled items of information. If the pupil has to think about his answer, the teacher is likely to have to think also—about what his next question should be. It is usually more important to keep the thinking going than to pronounce on it as right or wrong—not least because the latter is likely to terminate it.

More difficult issues arise when a decision has to be made as to whether to persist in questioning an individual pupil or to throw the question open to others. Save where the interaction is on a one-to-one basis, the questioning of one pupil is intended to provide instruction for the remainder of the class or group. Even the individual being questioned may gain more from the insights provided by another's answer. Clearly, judgement concerning balance of advantage is called for. If the pupils start to argue a point amongst themselves, the teacher has probably been very successful in establishing active thinking on the part of several pupils. The remaining task is to sustain and, where necessary, direct the discussion, and to do so unobtrusively. A quizzical look may prove more valuable than a question. Skilled questioning skills not only help pupils to learn, but help them to discover what learning is.

Integration of Knowledge

It might seem that, in the primary school where the teaching of virtually all subjects is usually undertaken by the same teacher, it would be easy to link together teaching in different subject areas. Yet in the observations it was a rare experience to record a serious effort to integrate what is taught in one area with that taught in another, even by the very simple means of recalling, while teaching in one area, what was taught in another. (Only 10% of teachers were observed to do so enthusiastically.) Transfer of knowledge and understanding from one context to another is widely regarded as one of the most necessary elements of learning. To establish the expectation that what is learned as arithmetic or science will be applicable to geography, or that knowledge of contemporary events may illuminate historical knowledge – or vice versa – is, surely, of fundamental importance?

'Project-work' was widely undertaken and it provided an opportunity for the integration of knowledge and skills. The integration that was found, however, was commonly superficial— and often little more than an easy way of finding something for pupils to draw.

Cooperative Learning

Projects also give an opportunity for cooperative work, and indeed this was quite often found. Unfortunately the cooperation most often involves sharing out different parts of a task rather than cooperative learning. Thus although some social training may be provided, the interplay of minds is frequently not facilitated. (Only 11% of the teachers observed encouraged co-operative learning frequently.)

Much of the difficulty seems to lie in a deeply entrenched view that, if pupils are set to work together, one or two will do all the work and thinking, and that the others will merely copy. (45% of the teachers observed sought to prevent all inter-pupil co-operation.) However, although it is clearly desirable to avoid virtual inactivity on the part of some pupils, it seems unwise to ignore the opportunities there are for pupils to learn from one another—though of course some monitoring of what is being learned is clearly essential if the transmission of error is to be avoided. The other factor that seems to inhibit teachers from encouraging or even permitting co-operative learning is the fear of losing disciplinary control. Such fear, however, smacks of defeatism. It is true that pupils may not spontaneously learn co-operatively but they can be trained to do so. It is merely one element in the process of learning to learn. Similarly skills in

29

working alone and using reference tools have to be taught and learned.

The mention of co-operative learning brings us back to the topic of learning in groups. Perhaps one of the prime teaching skills is to know how best to divide time between whole-class and group learning in such a way that

a) the teacher does not waste time repeatedly communicating the same thing to different individuals and groups

b) the pupil has the maximum individual stimulation and the maximum opportunity to inter-act with both teacher and other pupils

c) the pupil has adequate time to reflect on and consolidate what he has learned and to discover where he has difficulties with which he needs help.

Memorisation

The practice of the teachers observed made it clear that all saw some degree of memorisation as an essential part of school work. Where differences were observable, these related not to *whether* but to *how* and/or *what*.

Memorisation can usefully be divided into that which is the result of a direct endeavour to memorise and that which occurs incidentally in the course of experience or study. The former can be divided into rote learning on the one hand and meaningful memorisation on the other. Almost 30% of the teachers observed were judged to lay emphasis on the learning undertaken being based on understanding. It was, therefore, they who lay most emphasis on the teaching of concepts and on structuring the knowledge so that it would be likely to be remembered in a meaningful context. However, only about one sixth of them sought no rote learning. At the other end of the range, about 14% laid emphasis on rote to the virtual exclusion of any other form. The remaining 56% made some attempts to teach concepts etc, though rote learning, particularly of spelling and tables, was prominent.

It was in respect of arithmetic that attempts were most often made to teach concepts systematically, though there was often considerable dependence on a text-book for this work.

Reinforcement

Practice is generally recognised as a way of assisting memorisation of procedures such as those involved in specific types of arithmetic computation. Its role is thus analagous to that of rote learning, the latter being concerned with the memorisation of facts. Both are subject to excessive use even in cases where their employment may be justifiable. Thus some teachers caused pupils to practice arithmetical computations for excessive periods of time and long after successful performance was well established. It may be a convenient way of keeping pupils occupied but it is at the expense of other more valuable activities.

Feedback

Whatever the type of teaching adopted, pupils spend part of the time—often for a very substantial part of the time—working on their own, and teachers, without exception, provide them with some feedback so that they may know how far their attempts are successful. However, both the quantity and the type of that feedback varies greatly. The researchers found it useful, in the first place, to distinguish between *concurrent* and *retrospective* feedback – ie, between that given at the time the pupil is involved in the work and that given subsequently. Few would question the advantage of the former, for the help is given when problems or errors—if any—are occurring and when they are actively in the pupils' minds. The teacher's problem is the obvious one that it is difficult to provide concurrent feedback in the quantity required. It is, indeed, attempting to provide more than is practicable that leads to the phenomenon of queues of pupils awaiting correction of their work. There is a clear need for the teacher's time to be optimally used. Applying ticks and crosses alone is, in most cases, *not* optimal use of that time. That is a task pupils can do for themselves or for each other, if self-correction facilities are provided. The teacher's problem is to determine how best to locate those who require help and to provide it promptly. (See Figure 6)

Retrospective feedback, since it involves marking work, does, of course, give teachers a further opportunity to monitor progress, but, if it is to do more than this, means have to be found of providing further instruction of individuals or of groups of individuals with similar problems—again, something making considerable demands on teachers' time. If pupils give only a cursory glance at what a teacher has written, little purpose has been served.

From the point of view of the pupils, what matters is a suitable combination of concurrent and retrospective feedback—with the latter provided in such a way that they can recall what they were

31

Figure 6

A Cameo of Miss Ramsay*

Miss Ramsay was a very conscientious teacher who tended to overload herself with work but did not reflect this onto pupils, with whom she had a close relationship. She said that she found it necessary to use a fair number of groups in order that she could cater for all the pupils, whom she saw as being of diverse ability. (The class was a composite one.) She taught these groups individually and this cut down the time which she had available for concurrent feedback. Moreover, she herself did all correction of pupil work, something that she found very time-consuming (though much was done in evenings). Her doing so was not, she said, due to a lack of trust but because she saw it as a better way of maintaining control over pupil work and also because she did not consider the pupils to be very skilled at marking.

---

* Teacher 109 (cluster F) in *The Teacher's Craft*.

attempting to do at the time the work was undertaken. In the judgement of the observers, this was achieved by just under one half of the teachers observed—though less than 5% provided a level of feedback that seemed wholly inadequate.

One way in which many teachers sought to overcome the problem of how best to use available time for concurrent feedback was by moving around the class observing and deciding, on the basis of what they saw, whom to work with. Some, in addition, by having different groups of pupils engaged in different tasks only some of which were likely to give rise to need for their intervention, endeavoured to reduce the demand on themselves at any one time to manageable proportions.

There was, however, even amongst those who did move around the room providing feedback, considerable variation in how they did it. Some divided their time amongst many, giving, unavoidably, very little time to each. This probably served the purpose of keeping themselves informed on progress and perhaps of providing encouragement to pupils to work. On the other hand, it tended to be superficial. Other teachers preferred to spend substantial amounts of time working with individuals. This gave them the opportunity to give substantial help, but to only a few. The danger was of neglecting many others. There was also a danger of solving the same problem many times over, working with pupils one at a time. Those who managed to bring together those pupils requiring similar help were obviously making more effective use of their own time.

Testing

Whereas tests can, when marked, constitute feedback to pupils, they do not necessarily do so. Even specifically diagnostic tests may often constitute feedback to the teacher rather than the pupil. If this is so, the teacher requires to take action in informing the pupils concerned of what has been discovered and/or in undertaking specific remediation.

However, it should be noted that the research produced some evidence that in schools where the headteacher imposed a regime of weekly testing of arithmetic, probably with a view to securing effort and high levels of performance, the most obvious effect was that the teachers taught with a view to obtaining from their classes optimal performance in those tests. This they typically did by concentrating on mechanical means of securing correct answers (rather than on assisting their pupils to grasp the associated concepts) and by devoting much time to what was to be tested— something which in turn produced a restriction on the range of work that they attempted in other subject areas.

Teacher Sensitivity and Class Control

Class control is a management function. However, it is important to remember that, whenever management involves the management of people, it is more than a matter of organisation. Perhaps the most important skill in management is to be able to see situations through the eyes of those one is seeking to manage. To know (approximately at least) what a pupil would think and feel were one to interact with him in a particular way is, surely, a guide as to whether to do so in that way or to think of another more sensitive approach.

Being sensitive in this way does not necessarily imply being gentle or kind—thought it may do so—but acting with insight and thus with a greater likelihood of predicting the outcome. Take, for instance, Mrs McSween* who controlled with great skill a potentially difficult class of pupils from an area of notable social disadvantage: she was able to detect signs of trouble very early and defused the situations with great verbal skill. And, although she maintained a considerable distance from her pupils, she bestowed
* Teacher 79 (cluster H) in *The Teacher's Craft*.

33

her favours judiciously: she made it seem an honour to receive her attention, and this the pupils accepted.

Foreseeing probable outcomes is, of course, in itself inadequate. The small number of teachers observed who failed to establish anything better than short periods of precarious control (less than 2%) had doubtless witnessed many times the disintegration of control: they were manifestly apprehensive and were inclined to meet trouble half way. Unfortunately, their manner of confronting trouble, whether in the form of preemptive strike or verbal abuse, served only to guarantee the continuance or recurrence of the very trouble that they feared. They saw their pupils as adversaries. They appeared unable or unwilling to see the situation through their pupils' eyes. They appeared wholly unaware that hostility creates hostility. (A further 5% of the teachers observed showed similar characteristics, though to a less extreme degree. The amount of time and effort expended by them in maintaining control obviously impeded the teaching being attempted.)

Those who were generally successful in control did, of course, differ widely in their approach. Some, for instance, maintained steady dominance, though through a variety of means, some of them highly personal—as when for example, in the case of Mr Brown*, the teacher called the tune and was habitually "one move ahead of" pupils and was constantly "keeping them guessing". Others had about them "that that would be feared", something that caused most pupils most of the time to accept their dominance. (These teachers probably, in fact, resorted to punishment but rarely. Those who frequently used and/or threatened punishment were generally those who had attempted to achieve dominance but had not managed to do so). Yet other teachers had succeeded in establishing a situation that might be seen as a *partnership* between them and their respective classes. They had won both the hearts and minds of their pupils. They had established an atmosphere of joint endeavour, one largely free from any adversarial element. Their success in this owed much to both their personalities and to their skills in human relationships.

Teacher Sensitivity

Teacher sensitivity does, of course, have a wider role in teaching than that referred to in the context of class control. It does, moreover, involve more than anticipating likely reactions of others: it includes also rapid awareness of reactions other than those

* Teacher 80 (cluster L) in *The Teacher's Craft*.

expected, for the prediction of reactions to what one is about to do is rarely perfect, and certainly not uniform for every individual. Knowledge and understanding of each pupil is no less important than a general understanding of pupils.

Sensitivity to the attitudes and feelings of individual pupils is, in part, built on awareness of reactions, including some that are slight or partly hidden by the pupil. Knowledge of special circumstances affecting pupils is obviously helpful to the teacher in understanding pupil reactions, but so too is a basic relationship between teacher and pupil that permits the pupil to be open about what he feels. In this way both conflict and suppressed resentment can be minimised and differences between teacher and pupil 'negotiated' and resolved without conflict.

In classes where this had been achieved, there was an air of teacher and class 'pulling together'. The direction was agreed or accepted by all and pupils appeared typically self-assured. In contrast, where this had not been achieved, the self-confidence of at least some pupils was under threat and motivation endangered.

General Conclusions

Of those teachers observed, those that appeared to the author to be the most skilled differed considerably from one another in how they taught. It would, of course, be wrong to conclude from this that any sort of teaching is as good as any other. Rather, there would appear to be good grounds for considering that there are many ways of being a good teacher, that many teachers teach in ways that are far from optimal, and that even the very best teachers have scope for improving their performance. It is indeed one of the characteristics of those the author would judge to be excellent teachers that they did recognise the need to question constantly what they were doing, to monitor the effects of their own actions, and to arrive at new solutions. Rigidity of mind is the enemy of good teaching. Though 'successful' practice may be a useful guide, improving one's teaching does not lie in copying it but in analysing one's problems and finding ways of overcoming them as best one can. This is why this booklet not only does not, but cannot, prescribe solutions; it can only alert teachers to potential problems and provide some criteria for self-assessment. This booklet aims to be an aid to thinking, not a substitute for it.

Part of the explanation for this situation lies, of course, in the fact that different teachers necessarily have different priorities. Thus, for example, the need to develop in pupils independent learning skills differs greatly from class to class. Mrs McVey*, for instance, expended a great deal of effort in establishing in her P5 pupils habits of settling down to work alone. This she needed to do because the pupils she taught, who were drawn from an area of notable social deprivation, displayed a marked reluctance/inability to settle to any task for more than a brief duration. Her diagnosis of predominant need strongly influenced her priorities and hence how she taught. Those who taught self-assured pupils from homes that provided rich educational resources could, on the other hand, lay emphasis on other objectives. Such pupils might, for instance, require primarily strong intellectual challenge.

The need for treatment matched to individual needs calls, obviously, for a 'child-centred' approach. However, as has already been demonstrated, there is not a simple equivalence between child-centredness and the employment of 'group-methods'. Not all employment of group instruction or group work was in its effect child-centred, nor did whole-class teaching necessarily imply a lack of individualisation. In some classes 'teacher-centredness' and 'pupil-centredness' were not incompatible, for the teacher was able to be the pivot of activity and at the same time one who tailored each one-to-one interaction to the special needs of the individual. In short, 'teacher-centred' teaching—and indeed its supposed opposite, group methods—can imply either uniformity or diversity of treatment. Each may have certain inherent advantages and disadvantages, but the advantages and disadvantages arising from *how* they are employed are far more important than those that are inherent. What are essentially means to an end need to be seen as such. Means need constantly to be evaluated in the light of their actual, not their intended, outcomes. Even ends are not absolute: one may be achievable only at the expense of another. Circumstances may, and indeed should, influence the priorities to be attached to specific objectives and the sequence in which they are pursued. Effective teaching, is in short, a problem-solving activity: it cannot be rigid and unchanging. Good teaching practices cannot be had 'off the shelf': they arise from analysis of needs, from the monitoring of effects, and from imaginative and insightful attempts to meet ever changing and complex requirements.

* Teacher 37 (cluster N) in *The Teacher's Craft*.

APPENDIX

A Brief Outline of the Research Project

The teaching Strategies in the Primary School project arose out of a debate current in the early 70's concerning the relative merits of what was termed 'progressive' and 'traditional' teaching. The observations of classes that constituted the earliest phase of the research convinced the researchers involved that the distinctions implied by these two terms were not only poorly defined but also of little value since many important ways in which teachers differ from one another cut right across this dichotomy. Moreover, many of the more extreme features popularly associated with 'progressive' teaching proved to be outside the range of variation to be found amongst Scottish primary teachers. Accordingly, it was decided that what was required was a means of describing and recording a large number of characteristics in respect of which Scottish primary teachers had been observed to vary. To this end an observation schedule, the System for the Classroom Observation of Teaching Strategies (SCOTS) was devised and thereafter piloted on a sample of 138 teachers of classes P5, P6 and P7 in 30 schools in Edinburgh, Glasgow, the Lothians, Fife, Lanarkshire, Angus, Perthshire and Roxburgh. In the light of the data produced the SCOTS Schedule was revised.*

The schedule in its revised form was then used in the 1977/78 school session for the observation of the teaching of 128 teachers from 30 schools (mainly the same ones as in the pilot study), each teacher being observed five times for a period extending for approximately one quarter of a school day. Each of the 43 variables yielded a coding on a scale, usually a 5-point one. The resulting data were analysed with the purpose of collecting together in 'clusters' or groups those teachers whose teaching, as recorded, differed least. The result was the formation of 17 groups, each containing from 2 to 16 teachers with similar characteristics.

An attempt was made to measure the pupils' attitudes to school and their application to work when given a task that required them to attempt to understand some problem that caused them some

---

* The SCOTS Schedule is reproduced in Appendix A of *The Teacher's Craft*, and its items are discussed in detail in Chapter 3 of that book. In its revised form it covers 43 aspects of teaching that were deemed recordable and of potential importance.

degree of difficulty, both measurements being made both before and after they had been taught by the teacher concerned for 2-2½ terms. A similar attempt was made to measure relative attainment in arithmetic computation and in the concepts associated with the computation items.

It proved impossible to establish any clear-cut relationship between group-membership and changes in pupils as measured in respect of these things. Why this was so is discussed at length in *The Teacher's Craft*. Amongst the factors to be taken into account was the variation in the practices even of teachers classified together within a single group. The complexity of the patterns of variation found called into question the value of broad classifications of teachers. Classifications such as 'progressive' and 'traditional' clearly hide rather than reveal key differences.

What was observed enabled the researchers to obtain insights into the problems faced by teachers and into ways in which teachers seek to cope with them. What was 'learned' constitutes the foundation for the ideas and thinking presented in this booklet.